Contents

Halloween 4

Zombie finger puppet 6

Witch's broomstick 8

Pumpkin patch 10

RIP VIP invitation 12

Paper plate mummy hanging....... 14

Spooky sweetie tree 16

Bat hanging 18

Skeleton torch projection 20

Black cat lantern 22

Glossary and Index 24

Halloween

Halloween is a time of ghouls, ghosts and spooky goings on. Get into the spirit of things by getting crafty and making lots of 'frightfully' good things! Work your way through all the great projects in this book, creating monster makes to use as decorations, hangings and displays.

Each project in this book is easy to follow, and can be made in about 10 minutes. Every craft can be done lots of times, in different ways, using different materials, so there are plenty of ideas to keep you crafting for longer, too.

Pumpkin: pages 10–11

There is a small list of materials you will need for each project but don't feel like you need to stick to this exactly. Try swapping some things that are listed with other materials that you have already at home. Instead of using lots of felt to make the finger puppet on pages 6–7, you could use pieces of scrap fabric to make the body. Or you could use flattened cardboard boxes or cereal packets to make the torch projection on pages 20–21. So before you start shopping for lots of new art supplies, have a look at home and see what can be re-used or recycled.

10 Minute
HALLOWEEN
CRAFTS

ANNALEES LIM

First published in Great Britain in 2015 by Wayland

MIX
Paper from
responsible sources
FSC® C104740

FSC®
www.fsc.org

Editor: Elizabeth Brent
Craft stylist: Annalees Lim
Designer: Dynamo Ltd
Photographer: Simon Pask, N1 Studios

10 9 8 7 6 5 4 3 2 1

Dewey number: 745.5'941646-dc23
ISBN: 978 0 7502 8961 0
Library eBook ISBN: 978 0 7502 8785 2

Wayland is an imprint of Hachette Children's Group
Part of Hodder & Stoughton
Carmelite House, 50 Victoria Embankment, London EC4Y 0DZ

Printed in China

An Hachette UK company
www.hachette.co.uk
www.hachettechildrens.co.uk

Picture acknowledgements:
All step-by-step craft photography: Simon Pask, N1 Studios;
images used throughout for creative graphics: Shutterstock

Crafting can be messy, especially if you are using glitter or glues, so make sure you cover all your work surfaces with old newspaper or a plastic tablecloth before you begin. Always wash your hands after you have used glue to stop your works of art being ruined by sticky fingers, and always ask an adult to help you with scissors or sharp compasses.

Bat hanging: pages 18–19

Cat lantern: pages 22–23

Mummy: pages 14–15

Zombie: pages 16–17

Why wait? Get stuck in and be inspired by these projects to transform your home into the spookiest haunted house in town.

Zombie finger puppet

Bring this scary zombie to life when you put it on your finger, and plan your own zombie attack against other spirits and spooks.

You will need:

- Green, brown, black, white, yellow and red felt
- Scissors
- Fabric glue

Watch this step-by-step video of the zombie finger puppet being made!

1

Cut two felt rectangles that are large enough to go over your finger, and two smaller rectangles to make the arms.

2

Sandwich the arms inside the two larger rectangles of felt and stick in place using fabric glue.

Cut out some features to decorate your zombie. You will need black hair, brown shorts, two green hands, big yellow eyes and a black mouth.

Stick these to the green zombie base using the fabric glue.

Cut out lots of blood drops and splatters from the red felt and stick them all over your zombie.

Try making lots of different Halloween finger puppets. You could make werewolves and witches, or cats and bats – there are lots of options to choose from!

Witch's broomstick

Fill your ceiling with a whole cackling crew of these witches, and they'll look like they are soaring away to cast some spells.

1

Cut two brown pipe cleaners up into eight pieces of a similar length. Bunch them together and wrap the ends with another brown pipe cleaner. Leave the other end straight so it looks like the handle of a broomstick.

2

To make the witch's dress, fold a piece of A6 black card in half, then cut it in half. With the fold at the top, cut off two small triangles from one of the pieces, then cut a 2cm slit into the top.

3

Stick two googly eyes and some strands of purple wool onto the green pom-pom, to make the witch's head and hair.

4

To make the hat, cut out one circle and one semicircle of black card. Fold the semicircle into a cone, snip around the edge, and stick it to the card circle. Stick the hat to the head, then decorate the hat and dress with the stickers.

5

Bend a green pipe cleaner onto the broomstick to make the legs, then slide half a purple pipe cleaner through the slit in the dress to make the arms. Glue the dress over the broomstick and the head onto the dress.

Make your witch fly by tying some thin string or invisible thread to the broomstick and hanging it from the ceiling.

Pumpkin patch

Create a collection of playful clay pumpkins to decorate your Halloween table. You can write spooky messages, or the devilish delights you are serving up to your guests, on them.

1

Roll some orange clay into small balls of different sizes. Squish each one slightly between your thumb and forefinger to make them into pumpkin shapes.

2

Use the ruler to make indentations all around the pumpkins.

3

Make small triangles for eyes and a wavy line for a mouth out of the black clay, and press them onto the front of the pumpkins. Use the green clay to make the stems, and press into place.

4

Make small flags out of the cocktail sticks and strips of coloured paper, gluing each flag in place.

5

Press a flag into each pumpkin to make a hole. Bake the clay pumpkins as instructed on the packet, making sure you remove the cocktail stick flags before you put them in the oven.

Make holes right through each pumpkin using a cocktail stick to turn them into beads. They can be made into necklaces, bracelets or keyring charms.

RIP VIP invitation

When your guests receive these great gravestone party invites, they'll be sure to say yes to your ghoulish get-together!

1

Fold the A4 card in half and cut along the crease to make two A5 pieces. Fold both pieces in half to make two invites.

2

Take one of the invites and draw an upside down 'U' shape onto the top of the card using the pen.

12

3

Cut around the 'U' shape but instead of following the line exactly, make it jagged and uneven.

4

Use the pencil to colour in the front of the invite with hatched lines to make it look patchy. Then go around the edges with a black pen.

5

Cut out a pumpkin shape from the orange card and stick it to the front of the invite. Add details to the pumpkin using the black pen and then use the green and blue glitter glue to add some moss and the pumpkin's stalk.

Leave the invites plain, without any writing inside, and staple them onto some string to make spooky bunting.

Paper plate mummy hanging

This spooky hanging is perfect for decorating your house or your classroom. You could hang it in a doorway to welcome your guests to a Halloween party!

1

Staple the plates together as shown, and stick a loop of thread to the back of the top plate to make a hanging.

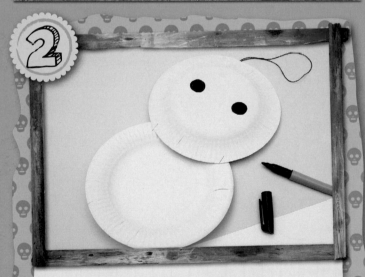

2

Use the black marker pen to draw eyes on the middle of the top plate.

3

Cut an A4 sheet of paper into four strips and fold each one up into a concertina.

4

Staple these onto the mummy to make arms and legs. Trim the ends of the concertinas so that they look like hands and feet.

5

Rip the tissue paper into small strips and glue them onto the head and body to look like layers of bandages.

Make a cardboard box tomb for your mummy to hang inside. Decorate the outside with yellow bricks and lots of hieroglyphics.

Spooky sweetie tree

The noise of the wind passing through the branches of trees can be pretty scary. Create your own haunted woodland scene, complete with spooky faces to hide wrapped sweet treats amongst.

You will need:

- Black paper
- Corrugated card (approx 10 x 15cm)
- Scissors
- A glue stick
- A toilet roll tube
- Brown paper
- Sticky tape
- A black pen
- Craft glue
- Small, wrapped sweets

1. Glue a piece of black paper onto the corrugated card using the glue stick.

2. Wrap the toilet roll tube in brown paper.

3

Rip more brown paper into 12 thick strips twice as tall as the toilet roll tube. Twist each strip loosely and then stick inside the tube, leaving a short end overlapping at the bottom and a long end at the top.

4

Draw a spooky face onto the front of the tree.

Once all the sweets have been eaten from the tree, you can replace them with the scrunched-up wrappers, if they are foil or shiny, or with some rolled-up bits of colourful tissue paper.

5

Splay the short ends of brown paper out, put lots of glue on them and then press them onto the black card base. These are the roots of the tree. Spread the branches out so they look as if they are swaying in the wind. Stick the sweets to the branches and scatter them round the roots, ready to serve.

Bat hanging

Bats like to hang around, especially in a large group. Each bat will take you about ten minutes to make, so if you have time, make a whole colony to fly through your classroom or bedroom.

You will need:

- Black and purple wool
- A ruler
- Scissors
- A fork
- A cocktail stick
- Black felt
- Fabric glue
- Two lolly sticks

Watch this step-by-step video of the bat hanging being made!

1

Cut a 10cm piece of wool and drape it through the middle gap of the fork.

2

Take another piece of wool and wrap it around the fork until you have covered all of the prongs.

Tie a loose knot around the middle of the fork to hold the wool in place, then slowly remove the wool from the fork. Tie the knot tighter so the wool turns into a pom-pom.

Put a cocktail stick through the middle of the pom-pom. Cut four matching wing shapes out of black felt and glue two onto each side of the pom-pom, sandwiching the cocktail stick in-between. Repeat steps 1—4 to make four more bats.

These mini makes can also be used as bat brooches.

Make the lolly sticks into a cross and glue in place. Tie the bats to it using some purple wool.

Just attach a safety pin to the underneath of a bat and wear it like a badge on your clothing.

Skeleton torch projection

Dim the lights before you start telling ghost stories, and turn on this terrifying torch to make spooky skeleton projections on the wall.

You will need:

- A large torch
- Black card
- Scissors
- A pencil
- Electrical tape

1

Cut out a piece of black card that is slightly bigger than your torch face.

2

Fold the piece of card in half and draw a long 'J' shape in the top section. Make sure the top of the 'J' touches the folded edge.

3 Add a set of sharp teeth underneath the 'J', starting from the fold.

4 Cut all the shapes out using your scissors.

5 Open out the card to reveal your skull cut-out. Hold this over the top of your torch, and stick it in place using the tape.

Use this technique to help tell spooky tales. Create the main characters of your story and use them to act out the scenes.

Black cat lantern

This lantern might not give off light, but it looks great and won't cast a shadow over your other decorations.

You will need:
- Black A4 card
- Scissors
- A ruler
- Sticky tape
- A glue stick
- Yellow stickers
- A black pen

1

Cut a piece of card in half, lengthways.

2

Fold one of the pieces in half again, lengthways, and cut slits at 2cm intervals all the way along the fold, making sure you don't reach the opposite edge.

Open this out, roll it into a tube and fix in place using sticky tape.

Cut a small strip from the rest of the black card and glue it to the top of the lantern.

Cut a cat's face, a tail and whiskers out of black card. Add black spots to the yellow stickers to make the cat's eyes. Stick all the features onto the lantern.

These lanterns look great as pumpkins too! Just use orange card instead of black, add a green handle to the top and draw on a scary face with a pen.

Glossary

bunting a row of cloth or paper decorations on a string
cackling laughing loudly
colony a group of animals that live very close to one another
ghoul an evil spirit or presence
hieroglyphics a form of writing using pictures, instead
of letters
spook a ghost
technique a way of doing something
tomb a chamber or vault for a dead body
werewolf a person who changes into a wolf at
full moon

Index

bats 7, 18-19

cats 7, 22-23

ghosts 4

ghost stories 20, 21

gravestone 12-13

haunted tree 16-17

hieroglyphics 15

mummy 14-15

pumpkins 10-11, 23

skeleton 20-21

werewolves 7

witches 7, 8-9

zombie 6-7